Fight Don't Faint

Strategies to Overcoming Opposition

Raquel Sylvester

Copyright © 2020 Raquel Sylvester

All rights reserved. No part of this book may be reproduced or transmitted in any form or by any means without written permission from the author.

Scriptures marked KJV are taken from the KING JAMES VERSION (KJV): KING JAMES VERSION, public domain.

T.A.L.K. Publishing
5215 North Ironwood Road, Suite 200
Glendale, WI 53217
talkconsulting.net

Title: **Fight Don't Faint:** Strategies to Overcoming Oppression
ISBN: 978-1-952327-25-4

Dedication

This book is for you, Mom! For instilling the love for people in me when I was a child. I never encountered you meeting a stranger. I watched you speak to everyone that you walked by. Regardless if it was in the grocery store, the mall, or even the doctor's office. Your gentleness taught me that fighting is more than an aggressive way of winning, but that it is an aggressive way to express love for myself and others. I will always be your "Baby Girl," "Brat," and "Rocky."

Fight Don't Faint
Strategies to Overcoming Opposition

Acknowledgements 9
Foreword 11
What's the Plan? Make it Count! 15
Let's Start Training 23
Protect Yourself 33
Stand Your Ground and Don't Be Scared 39
Know Your Opponent – For My Bible Readers 45
Rest Breaks 53
Stay Focused 59
Don't Let the War Wounds Fool You 63
Tender Spots 67
Don't Take it Personal 71
What's Next? It's in Your Words 75
From My Heart To Yours 79
A List For My Ladies 83
A List For My Fellas 85
A Prayer For The Fighter In You 87

Acknowledgements

I must start by thanking my four beautiful children. Each one of you played such an important role during my writing process. Akeem, your consistent words of encouragement kept me going on days I wanted to cry. You made sure that I paid attention to every detail and your nightly phone calls brought me comfort and relief. May your head always be lifted. Jona'e, my hype-girl, you reminded me daily of how proud you were of me, so I take this time to say I'm proud of you too! Continue to congratulate others, and you will always have something to be congratulated for. My middle child-Correna. Thank you for reminding me to breathe and take breaks. I pray that you always breathe through whatever challenge comes your way and know that you can accomplish anything you put your mind to. Last but not least, my prince-Du'Sean. It is your energy that keeps me youthful. Your "snuggles" make me smile, and your laugh keeps me balanced. I love you all.

To my big sister, Daphne, as I aspired to be like you, you made sure that I stayed true to myself. You made sure that I walked in God's purpose for my life and not the ideas of others. You fulfilled your duty as "big sis," and I love you for doing so.

To my Pastor and 1st Lady, Marlon, and Kimberly Lock, you noticed, acknowledged, and cultivated the spiritual warrior in me. Your patience is impeccable. It has been an honor to learn and serve in the ministry with you. You taught me to walk in the Believers Authority, and through this series of teachings, this book is produced. I won't faint because I am a Believer!

Last but not least, to the Cunningham Girls, also known to me as the Top 10, who were born to the marriage of James and Opal Cunningham. Vikki, Rena (mom), Freddie, Barbara, Rita, Marilyn, Diane, Linda, Patricia, and Bridget. All of you have (has) a strength that I was able to pull from at one time or another in my life. I have watched each one of you fight through some challenging times that would cause the average person to faint. But you did not, and for that, you will always be my Top 10!

Foreword

It is with extreme honor that I write the foreword for my sista and friend, Raquel Sylvester. Her book entitled "Fight, Don't Faint" is a testament to her character and willingness to fight through life's most challenging moments. I met Raquel approximately eight years ago; we are both members of Unity Gospel House of Prayer Church. She has been a faithful member and has always had a willing heart to serve and assist in the ministry. She is a minister that preaches the word of God, and she also is a part of the children's ministry. Over the years, our relationship outside of the church walls has grown dramatically. I can recall to my mind how many times Raquel has invited me over for dinner in the past, and she still does that even today. She has had some of the best fish fry's, and she loves bringing people together. This speaks volumes of her because she always has an open door for people. If she has it, she doesn't mind sharing. Raquel has been incredibly supportive and encouraging with my endeavors as well as the endeavors of others. Anytime I have had an event, she has shown support in some form. I have watched Raquel at a distance fight through some challenging moments in her life, but she never fainted. God's plans are for us to prosper, but it does not mean that we are exempt from the challenges in life. When Raquel told me she was going back to school for her Bachelor's degree in special education, I was excited for her. My excitement was not because of the pursuit of a degree but because of what the achievement would mean to so many others that were watching. Her achievement meant that despite the beginning of her life's journey, she still had the power to write a different narrative for her life. During her return to college, there were times when Raquel was frustrated about the amount of work that was on her plate, but what I remember most is how she prayed and pressed her way to the finish line. Raquel is a faithful servant of God, and I can attest to that, as evidenced by her Christian walk. She holds the titles of minister, wife, mama, daughter, sister, teacher, student, and friend. With these titles, she's faced moments that, without God, she might have fainted, but the God in her allowed her to fight. Fight through the moments of disappointment. Fight through the moments of embarrassment. Fight through the moments of doubt and fight through the moments of despair. I have had the pleasure of watching her in action as a mama. She loves her children and genuinely wants the best for them. Her children know the Lord, which is evidence of the time she invested in them. She has taught them about God, so when they have their challenging moments, they have a point of reference to refer to. Raquel has a love for God's people; she is truly about her Father's business. As a minister, she is on the front line, and as a front liner, sometimes injuries do occur. What I love about her is that she has never let an injury stop her from doing what God has called her to do. Raquel is bold for God, and she walks in her God-given authority. She has had impeccable growth over the years, and she is an inspiration to herself, children, and everything that's an extension of her. I know God is well pleased with her, and her walk is marvelous in His eyes. Fight, Don't

Faint is not just a book, but it is a tool for life. This book will bless those who read it. As a reader, you will not only read about Raquel's testimony as she takes you on a journey sharing intimate details about her life and the moments where she almost fainted, but you will walk away with tools that will help you on your journey to fight in a world that wants you to faint.

Dr. Darlene C. Beck
Owner/Operator of Setting The Bar, L.L.C.

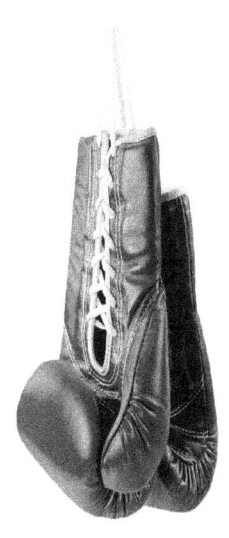

What's the Plan? Make it Count!

Have you ever felt like Sophia in the movie Color Purple when she said, "All my life I had to fight?" Well, I have. Maybe not for the same reasons as Sophia did. But I sure had to fight. Middle school was the roughest for me. I attended a creative arts school in the middle of "Lapham Projects" and "Hillside Projects" in Milwaukee, Wisconsin. These projects were designed for affordable housing. They were called "projects" because they were construction "projects" in undeveloped areas designed to keep poor people segregated from the middle and upper class. I'm sure you already know what happens when you put a huge number of poor people together, without resources.

Exactly, not much good. So, there were gangs and poverty on both sides of my school. Not only were these projects full of gangs and poverty, but there were also drugs, drug users, and prostitution, all of which I was unfamiliar with. Don't get me wrong, there may have been some of these things going on around me, but my mom kept me pretty sheltered. I was her baby girl, and you know how that goes. She did not let me see, hear, or do much. Most of the students that attended school with me lived in one or the other project. I didn't live in the school's neighborhood, so the only time I saw my peers were when we were at school. Still, it seemed like every week, a girl from one of the projects wanted to physically fight me for some strange reason. And so, I did what my momma told me, I "put my dukes up," and I fought back. As a matter of fact, my momma told me if I was outnumbered, to always get the first lick in and make it count! Hmmm, make it count?

Making it count meant I needed to strategize. How and where I hit was important to not losing the fight. I could not just swing my fist and hope for the best. I needed to make sure that even if I did not win, these girls would not want to mess with me again. Needless to say, I won some fights, and I lost some. The point is I either fought back or got beat up.

My MaMa Taught Me How To Fight

I remember one day, at the age of 7 years old, my mom sent me to the "corner store" to buy a couple of things. The corner store was only half of a block away, so she thought I was mature enough to take her list and get what she wrote down. We lived on 33rd and North Avenue. This was not the worst of neighborhoods, but it definitely was not the best either. It was normal for a kid to go to the store with a list from their parents back then. While I was on my way to the corner store, three girls passed by that looked like they were up to no good. I was a little nervous to walk past them, but I did anyway, and low and behold, they started walking behind me. While they were walking behind me, they were taunting me. I did not stop. I just kept walking. They called me names in hopes of getting a response, but I did not turn around until I got to the store.

When I got to the store, I did not go in. Instead, I thought, I better say something back to the girls, or they were going to think I was scared of them. As I was talking to them, I turned around and started walking back home. I figured let me get as close to my momma as possible in case they tried to beat me up. She would hear me. Well, they didn't get a chance to beat me up. I made it home, and of course, I told my momma everything that happened. Now I'm not sure if she was mad that I didn't bring her items back or because the girls were mean, but she put her shoes on and walked me right back down to where the girls were. I was so nervous 'til sweat was probably dripping down my face. I did not know what she was going to do. Well, she walked up to the girls and said, "Which one of y'all wanna fight my daughter?" My eyes got so big, and I thought they were going to pop out my head. Of course, neither of them said anything, and I was glad. My mama and I went into the store, bought the items that were on her original list, and came out. I never had a problem with those girls on the block again. Now I'm sure the girls were not afraid of me, but I was no longer afraid of them either. The lesson my mama taught me was to never be scared, even if it seemed like I was outnumbered. At that moment, at the young age of 7 years old, she taught me to face my fears and Fight!

Now, schoolyard or adolescent neighborhood fighting was not the only thing that caused me to put my dukes up and fight. At about eight years old, my mom introduced me to church. We were members of God's Holy Tabernacle Church. It was right around the corner from where we lived. It was a family-oriented church, and we soon were part of the family. I grew up believing that Hell is real, and if you don't want to go there, then you don't sin. No boyfriends, no going to the clubs, no secular music, I couldn't wear certain clothes. You get the picture. I loved going to church. What I saw in church, I wanted to do. I saw people as young as 16 years old getting married, and I thought it was so cool. To me, being married and in your own house was pleasing God, so I got married at an incredibly early age too. Needless to say, the marriage only lasted two years. After that, I waited fourteen years to try the marriage thing out again, and guess what? That marriage lasted three years. I was now a mama of two beautiful children and single. Chileeeee, I had to fight to keep food on the table and clothes on their backs. Most importantly, I had to make sure a strong spiritual foundation was laid for my children no matter what had taken place. Through all of this, thoughts crossed my mind that questioned my worth.

Two failed marriages, two children, and living paycheck to paycheck. Where do I go from here? Would I ever have a successful marriage? Shoot, did I even want to try the marriage thing again? Who would want me now that I had "baggage?" All questions that I pondered daily. Life became heavy, and sometimes it felt unbearable. I did not want to be another statistic, but here I was, broke, busted, and disgusted. I was trying to make ends meet, with my babies looking at me in the face expecting nothing to change. They did not understand that there were no longer two incomes in the house and that things definitely were different.

The guilt and shame of my past had almost gotten the best of me. Then all at once, I remembered everything I was taught as a child. I remembered whose child I was. I belonged to God. See, sometimes life has a way of making you forget where you came from, especially after a tragedy or disappointment occurs. But I remembered hearing Him speak to me at the age of sixteen. I remembered He told me that I was His child and that He had chosen me! I remembered that "greater was He that was in me than He that was in the world" (King James Version, n.d., 1 John 4:4), and immediately I stopped thinking about opposition. I started thinking about winning the fight the way my mama taught me.

Opposition is inevitable. There will be struggles that come up often for some and less frequent for others. The Bible says, "That it is impossible but that offenses will come: but woe unto him through whom they do come" (King James Version, n.d., Luke 17:1). Some opposition will come through people (as most of mine did), and sometimes it will just be the continual cycle of what seems like, disparity. Just know, my cherished reader, that although opposition is inevitable, you can win the fight.

Why Fight?

I've often heard that we are our own worst critics. At times when life presents heaviness or opposition, we fold. We make up our mind that because unfortunate situation after situation presents itself to us, there is no need to challenge it, but that's not true. Maybe you lost the last fight, and now the spirit of defeat is playing with your mind. *Yes, I said, playing with your mind.* I said, playing with your mind because our mind is a battlefield. We can choose to *play* or *fight.* It depends on how you analyze situations. It is important that we choose to fight. If we choose to play, then life becomes a game, and defeat is entertained, and ain't nobody got time for that! I'm reminded of the movie titled Mahogany. In the voice of Diana Ross, "I'm A Winner Baby!" Yes, and you are too. There is strength in you that you have not even discovered. The only reason you have not discovered it is that you forgot who and whose you are. You forgot that you hold power to your success. You forgot that just because it didn't work last time doesn't mean it won't work this time, and you lost sight of the finish line. But that's okay. We are going to take this journey together.

After going through situation after situation, I learned that winning requires a strategy, and I began to think of strategy as training. There were steps that I was going to need to implement if I wanted to win. Like a boxer, they do not just get in the ring and win a fight. Neither will you. If you would allow me the opportunity to present these strategies to you, I guarantee by the end of this book, not only will your head be lifted up, but just like a boxer who wins a fight, you will come out with your hands up. Throughout this book, I will use the correlation of a heavyweight boxer to a person who is fighting to live (that's you). I am a visual learner, and my hope is that you will get a clear picture of what victory looks like through these correlations. I have also chosen to include *A song for the moment* before each chapter. These songs are included to set the tone for each chapter. When I was growing up, Saturday mornings were for deep cleaning. My mama would turn on the music and get started. It was something about listening to music while you cleaned. It seemed as if we did a more thorough job because the music had set the tone. As you prepare for each strategy, please, take the time to listen to the song first. Victory is waiting.

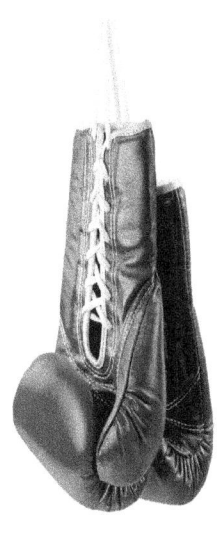

Let's Start Training

The Regimen Step 1: Build Strength and Speedy Reflexes

As I began to go through my second divorce, I started looking at life differently. I became more focused. I began to seek God for direction. My prayers became intentional. My ears were open. I began to surround myself with individuals who would add and not take away from what had already been disrupted. I also started reflecting on my childhood. I grew up in a family full of women, but these were not your average women. These women were fighters. My mama had nine sisters, no brothers, and my mama was the second oldest. Which meant she was often in charge. Yes, my grandparents, James and Opal Cunningham, had ten daughters! If you messed with one of them, you had to answer to all of them. Of course, the apple does not fall far from the tree. It was because of the family connection that I had the "fighter" mentality already in me. One day in my prayers, God allowed me to compare fighting in the physical sense to fighting in the spiritual sense. Through scriptures and life, he showed me how to get through what seemed to be a repeating cycle of unfortunate situations. He showed me a heavyweight champion at the end of a fight, with his hands up in the air. I used the image of the heavyweight champion to give me the ammunition I needed. See, in the world of boxing, there is a regimen used to prepare the body before getting in the ring. One thing a boxer must-do before getting in the ring is to build strength and speedy reflexes. A boxer knows that he or she cannot become complacent. They must be able to respond quickly to their opponent. Well, it is the same in life.

I realized that I had to think like a boxer and be quick with my responses but not react impulsively for me to get through the many challenges that were presenting themselves. There is a difference. Moving quickly can be beneficial, but reacting hastily can cause damage. Sometimes in life, after being hurt or disappointed, time after time, you begin to build a wall around your heart, and it becomes hardened. That is what happened to me. I had that "I'ma show you better than I can tell you" spirit. Well, that is called being impulsive. God showed me that was not His way, nor was it the way to win. I needed to become strong in Him. Let us go to the Word of God. Ephesians 6:10 reads, "Finally, my brethren, be strong in the Lord, and in the power of his might." Reading this let me know that if I wanted to build strength, I could not rely on my own strength, but I had to press into His strength. My strength would have me swearing, snapping, and acting unseemly, which afterward would result in confusion and anger. God's strength came with peace and a sound mind. This is what I needed. This is also what you will need. Let's face it. If we are going to face opposition, then we might as well face it with harmony, right? We can only do this by acknowledging that we need God's help. Listen, it takes a whole lot of weight off you when you let him help. Who wants to walk around loaded with weights? Not me. Not you either.

The Regimen Step 2: Endurance

Another major component of training for a fight is endurance. Boxers use battle ropes to help with fatigue management. Continually swinging the ropes in various patterns elevates the heart rate and forces the core to maintain stability. Listen, my beloved, I know that you will become fatigued at some point. No one is expecting you to be superwoman or superman. Therefore, you will need to have a system in place to help when you have those moments of exhaustion. Just like the boxer uses battle ropes to build endurance, start your day off and speak daily affirmations to remind yourself how strong you are so that when situations arise, you have thoughts to overpower the opposition. Affirmations remind you to keep going. They keep you focused on the possibility and not defeat. In the church-world, they call this "speaking over yourself." For instance, I would post affirmations on my bathroom mirror, so when I woke up, the first thing I would see were words that said, "You Are Enough." Your affirmations can be short or long; just make sure you are building yourself up during this training process.

Next, you will need to take a step back and evaluate the opposition that has you stuck. You did not get where you are overnight. A lot has transpired. What is it that has you in your feelings? Or that has you crying. Or that is stopping you from seeing the best in yourself. This is the time to consider, is it a person? Are you in your own way? Or is it a lack of knowledge? While evaluating these situations allows you time to get your plan together, you start to build a sense of stability (endurance).

The most assured way to gain stability is to accept what has taken place in your life, allow yourself to go through feeling whatever emotion attached to the process, and then press past it. It's okay to feel. This was hard for me. I would often press past situations but not allow myself to feel. At first, I thought if I allowed myself to feel, then I would get stuck in the situation. Then I realized that if I pressed past it without allowing myself to feel, it would probably come back up again, and in moments that had nothing to do with the actual issue. For example, when I went through my first divorce, I was young and free. I went on about my business like I had not lost anything.

The reality was, I was disappointed, hurt, and confused. I would even add that there was some "church-hurt" involved. Remember, I did what I saw others doing, but it did not work out for me. I did not understand why it did not because my intention was to do what I thought was right. Because I did not allow myself to go through the feelings when I got a divorce, the feelings came up in a relationship years down the road. Do not let this be you. When you are evaluating your life, allow yourself time to process. You do not have to linger in the moment. Just accept what has happened, do not beat yourself up, but realize a brighter day is ahead. We are still in training. Let us add one more thing to our regimen before we dive into our strategies.

"I'm no longer accepting the things I cannot change.

I'm changing the things I cannot accept."

Angela Davis

The Regimen Step 3: Increase Muscle

Boxers use what are called Slam Balls to increase muscle. In this journey called life, you will also need to increase muscle. Why? Because the more muscle you have, the less body fat. We all know that too much body fat causes high blood pressure, and high blood pressure causes strokes, and this is not something you want to deal with on top of life's challenges, right? You don't want extra "fat" on your body. You want muscle. Now I'm sure you're saying, what can I do to build "muscle" in the face of opposition? Well, the first thing is you must realize that winning requires strength. You must dig deep within yourself and pull out the heavyweight champion. You must understand that winners don't stop fighting until the bell rings, and then you must gird up the loins of your mind. Building muscle requires you to increase your training regimen. What you are doing now is good, but now is the time to "level-up." That means find yourself a class or two on leadership or growth.

That means going to seminars or conferences where like-minded individuals are. You may have attended one conference last year, increase it to 3 this year. You may have attended one professional development session this year; increase it to 3 next year. Start adding credits to your transcript by taking a class here and there. The credits will add up, and so will your muscle. Increasing your regimen means doing something different. You cannot expect different results if you keep doing the same thing. Remember, we are going for the championship, so we must train like a champion. In the process of building muscle, you might even want to start making a list of "fat" that you are losing. The relationships you cut-off, the places you stopped going to, and the distractions that were just excess weight. When you look at that list, you will realize how many pounds you have lost. The new you is looking thinner, and the muscle is starting to bulge out! After a while, your confidence will increase, and you will realize it's only up from here.

I once read an anonymous quote that said, "The strongest people are not those who show strength in front of us but those who win battles we know nothing about."

After writing my list, losing excess fat, and building some muscle, I went through a time where I felt isolated. Now that I had disconnected unhealthy relationships and was self-evaluating, my "friend-circle" had become more like a "corner." I was doing a lot of work, and I did not want to overwhelm the few friends that I kept with my heavy load. So here I was, fighting on the inside, and no one knew. Before I go any further, let me say this. If you are suffering from some sort of physical or mental abuse in silence, that is different. I would encourage you to tell someone else. I was not suffering from either of those. I was fighting what I now know was a fixed fight. I was trying to get from defeat to victory. Not sharing with friends or family allowed me to build a closer relationship with my heavenly Father. My prayer life became intentional. I realized the plans that my heavenly Father had for me were not to fail but to prosper. I started spending more time listening than speaking. The more I prayed, the more direction I received. As I was building this relationship, I wanted to make sure that my prayers were not selfish, but this was not the time for me to think about anyone else. I had to get myself together first. All I knew was that I could not give up, and it was going to take supernatural strength for me to win. This win was for the team, not just me.

I knew telling everybody else was not going to help me at this moment. I had my children to think of. They needed me to fight. So, I put my trust in Him, not in people, and things changed. He did not allow me to look like what I was going through. I started building more and more muscle because now I was not relying on my own strength or the strength of my friends or family, but rather, I depended on my Father's strength. Just like earthly parents, when children are struggling to get their heads above water, they come to the rescue with strategies that result in a lifeline. Let us look at some strategies that I learned as I was building this intimate relationship with God.

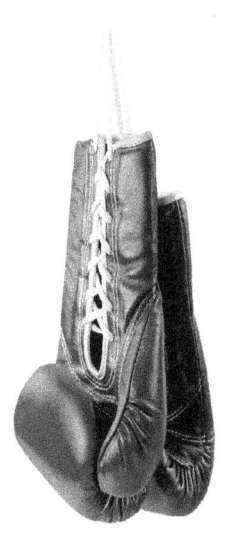

Strategy #1
Protect Yourself

A Song for this Moment:

James Fortune and FIYA- Let Your Power Fall (feat: Zacardi Cortez)

One of the first strategies that God began to reveal to me was that I had to learn to protect myself if I wanted to win the fight. Now that I was building a more intimate relationship with God, and my prayer life was more intense, things were clearer. Of course, they would be. Here I was, not sharing with others, and I had to talk to somebody, so I just talked to God. One day while in prayer, He showed me that there was some equipment that I would need to protect myself.

During that time, I read a scripture in the Bible that said, "Put on the whole armor of God, that ye may be able to stand against the wiles of the devil (Ephesians 6:10)." This blew my mind. Not only did I need to protect myself, but I also came to the knowledge of who I was protecting myself from. Yes, I had to finally acknowledge that some of the opposition I was facing was because of the purpose that God had for me. I was experiencing spiritual attacks to distract me from that life of peace and blessings that were promised to me. Once I realized this, my entire life changed. Once you realize this, yours will too. You see, the wiles of the devil meant that the devil had cunning strategies that he would use to manipulate or persuade me into doing or thinking that I was defeated. Now I told you earlier that I came from a family of fighting girls, so defeat was not an option. I needed to do something different. I had to put on the fighting gear. As I continued searching the scriptures, they continued to show me what fighting gear I needed. At one point in my life, I thought money was my protection. I thought that if I had a few dollars to do this or that, or if I had a better job that paid more money, I would be protected. I was wrong. I needed spiritual protection. If, by chance, you think like I once did, take this opportunity to reset.

Let me use the example of a boxer again; when they get in the ring, they have several pieces of equipment that are used for protection. A few of the things they use are mouth guards, gloves, and groin protectors. Let us talk about the mouth guard. The mouth guard covers the mouth. Listen to me. Our mouths need to be protected when we are trying to win because sometimeeeeee we can talk our way into more trouble. You must be slow to speak if you plan on winning. Have you ever been in a situation and you knew you were right, so you felt compelled to state your case? You knew you were right, so "they" were going to hear what you had to say? Welp, if you have not been there, I have. I did not understand what it meant to bridle my tongue. It did not matter how many people tried to explain it. If I was right, you were going to know it. But, when I started training to win, I learned to count to 10 before I responded. This would give me time to soften my words or not use them at all. I learned that it was okay not to respond to every situation that challenged me. This one was hard for me, but I did it, and you can too.

In addition, there are gloves. Boxers wear gloves to protect their hands and fingers from becoming broken during the fight. You will need your hands during this journey because there will be some days you will need to lift them in worship. Lifting your hands in worship, symbolically shows that you acknowledge you need God. And, through Him, your strength will remain. You do not have time to be without strength, so protect your hands because you are about to get in the ring. The hands are also used to plow. There is much work to do, still some things to be plucked up and plucked out, so you need your hands. You will also need them to gather the harvest you are about to have. Do not think you are doing all this work, and there is no return. Oh no! Your return will be unbelievable, so you might as well start visualizing your victory.

Equally important is the groin protector, which covers the most sensitive part of a boxer's body. I learned that one of the most sensitive parts of our body is our heart. It is the center of who you are. You must guard it because everything you do from here on out will flow from it. What you let affect it will also affect your ability to win. You must be careful not to allow your heart to be contaminated with things such as unforgiveness or grudges. Please note, it will take forgiveness to get through this process. But do not look at forgiveness as a weakness. It's for the protection of your heart. If you do not forgive others or you hold a grudge toward someone, how do you expect God to forgive you? The same grace you want extended to you, you will need to extend to others, or your heart will become hardened and stony. Stones are heavy to carry.

If you think about it, a boxer does not get in the ring with a lot of clothes on. He must be light-weighted-so get rid of those stones. People with stony hearts become bitter, cold, and unwilling to change. If you are unwilling to change, then you will be stuck in the same place forever. Unforgiveness will also hinder your prayers, and you want every single prayer to be heard and answered. You want a pure heart, so you must protect it by letting go of any hurt, guilt, or shame that may have been caused by someone else.

The Holy Spirit is your divine protection. Once you have accepted Jesus, He will be your protection when the jabs of opposition are thrown at you. When troubles come in like a flood, He will be there to block you from dangers seen and unseen. Another way the Holy Spirit protects you is by giving you the gift of discernment to aid you during your fight. He will not let anything sneak up on you. That is the kind of protection you need! Now you may be saying to yourself that you are not a super religious person, so how will the Holy Spirit protect me? Well, the first thing you need to do is understand the Holy Spirit is a gift. Gifts are given. Gifts are not always earned. This gift is given by your Creator, who knew you would need it and thought you were worth it. It is a gift for all believers. So, receive it. Don't forfeit it. Keep it and use it. It is the most precious gift you will ever receive. Secondly, being religious is not necessary but being open-minded and developing a spiritual relationship with God is. This process may require separation from people at times. If you think about it, when a boxer is in the ring, there is the boxer, the opponent, and the referee. You can't take family into the ring with you. You can't take your friends into the ring with you either. But as long as your referee is the Holy Spirit, you are all good. Bottom line, you cannot get into the ring unprotected. If you do, your opponent will whoop a fit on you.

There is another component to protecting yourself. This component includes love. The boxer gets in the ring wearing the bare minimum. He has protective gear, shorts, and shoes. There is a message in the shoes. What do you have on your feet when fighting? I was taught as a teenager that I must walk in love. Walking in love meant that people could see God in me. It was not hard for me to love people, but it was difficult for me to love someone who had mistreated or caused harm to me. I remember sitting at my grandmama's kitchen table one day. My great-aunt, who was 98 years old at the time, had taken the train all the way from Oklahoma to visit us in Milwaukee. I thought that was heroic of her and I must sit and have a talk with her.

Growing up, I was always intrigued by the conversations of my elders. While sitting there with her, I asked her, "what is the most important thing to do in my Christian journey?" Her reply was, "Forgive Others." She told me that was the love of God. What she did not know was that I was in the middle of a divorce, and I was struggling to let go of hard feelings. The Bible speaks about loving your opponent (enemies). In order to forgive them, you must possess love. Possessing love will allow you to look past others' faults. This is crucial. You want to look past their faults because you want to see your victory. Sometimes people do not even know why they behave in certain ways. That is how you know this fight is spiritual. If you spend time hating them or trying to figure out why they did this or that, you are giving them power. I remember having this very conversation with one of my mentors Kimberly Lock, years ago.

I just could not figure out why a certain person was treating me a certain way, and my heart was starting to feel ill toward them. She told me it really did not even matter why, but what did matter was that my heart was pure. I declare and decree that after this day, you will not give any more power to your opponent by carrying stones that were not intended for you to carry. You will love people in spite of, and you will be free indeed. In loving your opponent, you do not have to be gullible, but you do want to use wisdom to get to the next level. Focus on things that are lovely and true while God guards (protects) your heart. It's a Win-Win situation!

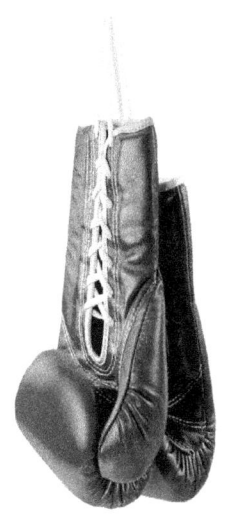

Strategy #2
Stand Your Ground and Don't Be Scared

A Song for this Moment:

1 2 3 Victory- by Kirk Franklin

In the world of boxing, a true boxer knows to stay away from the corner. There are four corners in a ring. When you go to the corner, it is easy for your opponent to attack and hard for you to get out. Most people go to the corner when they are scared because it gives you a sense of safety, but a sense of safety will give you a false reality. I know you may be saying, "I would rather be safe than sorry," but I would like to think that you would rather be "sure" than sorry. The corner is a trap. Sometimes your defense mechanism will make you want to go to the corner.

Let's talk about the four corners of the ring for just a moment. In each corner, we will use bad habits that tempt us when we are scared. In corner #1, overeating. Yes, we all have guilty pleasures but let's not make binge eating one of them. Overeating causes the stomach to expand beyond its normal size to adjust to a large amount of food. The expanded stomach then pushes against other organs. When this happens, you become uncomfortable. Then you become sluggish and tired, which is not good if you are planning to win the fight.

In corner #2, alcohol abuse. This seems to be one of most people's "go-to" when they are trying to escape the realities of life. Too much consumption of alcohol causes drunkenness. If you've seen a drunk, you know their speech is slurred, their gate is off-balanced, and they do not normally think straight. You will need to be sober during this process because the Bible says to be sober and of a sound mind. You will not have time for delayed reactions caused by drunkenness. Yes, a strong drink may take the "edge" off temporarily, but you want permanent solutions, not temporary fixes.

In corner #3, substance abuse. Anxiety, stress, and depression are all elements of everyday life. If you use drugs to cope or feel a sense of safety, you are likely self-medicating to mask the emotions attached to these elements. Take the mask off. You don't need it. There are long-term health problems associated with this behavior. Your body is a temple-it is your home. Take care of it, respect it, and treat it well. You will need it in it's best shape when you are in the ring.

Corner #4, now this one is one of the most common bad habits that I had to get rid of. Emotional shopping. Yes, I confess. On days when I felt emotionally distressed or I had a "bad" day, I would shop. There is something about a new pair of shoes when you are feeling scared or anxious. I don't know about you, but it sure made me feel better at the moment with a trip to the mall to spend money that I didn't have. Yep, that was me. But guess what? It's a trick too! There are disadvantages to emotional shopping. Your opponent wants you broke and feeling guilty, so you are unfocused. He wants to distract you. You must stay in control of the ring.

Winning is not for the faint at heart. The reality is, there may be some bloodshed. You may even get hit in the face a couple of times. I do not know one person who entered a fight and never got hit. Winning does not mean that you need to be aggressive; it means you must think. You cannot think if you are scared. Stay in the center of the ring. How do you stay centered? First, you must find out the times when you are most uncentered. Then, you reground your thoughts. At one point in my life, I thought that I could not speak up for myself because I was a Christian. I thought that I could not defend myself; I did not have the right to push back, so I found myself in the corner of the ring. As I began to build my relationship with God, I read in the Bible that the kingdom suffereth violence and the violent take it by force (Matthew 11:12).

Now do not get me wrong. There is a right and a wrong way to do everything so let us take it by force the right way. Let us not go knocking people upside the head because they did us wrong and say the Word of God told us to. "Take it by force" means, sometimes you must force yourself to get up. Sometimes you must force yourself to dust yourself off. Sometimes you may even have to force yourself to fight back but guess what, my love, even when it is forced, it still counts! When I was a teenager, I heard my mama say that the race isn't given to the swift, nor the battle to the strong, but it is given to the ones who endure to the end. So even if you must fight scared, do it scared then! Even if you are shaking in your boots. Even if tears are rolling down your face and you can barely see, just stay on your feet and stay away from the corner.

"I don't run away from a challenge because I am afraid. Instead, I run towards it because the only way to escape fear is to trample it beneath your foot."

Natalie Comaneci

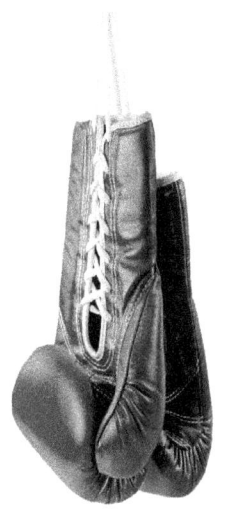

Strategy #3
Know Your Opponent – For My Bible Readers

A Song for this Moment:

We Gon Be Alright- by Tye Tribbett

Picture a boxing ring. In a fair fight, there are two fighters. Each fighter has a cornerman. The corner-man is only used to train or assist. The cornerman cannot instruct, but he helps you to watch your opponent so that when you are in between rounds, he can inform you of your opponent's tricks. You are not in this fight alone. Maybe you've been disappointed a few times by people, and you decided that you don't need anybody else. Can I offer a suggestion right here? Although you don't want to solely depend on others, as you develop knowledge and wisdom, you will want to get yourself a corner-man or woman if you plan to come out of the ring in one piece.

Your corner-man or woman can be your mentor, a life coach, your therapist, a prayer partner, or even your Pastor. You see, the corner-man will see attacks before you see them; therefore, your opponent cannot sneak up on you. The corner-man will remind you to rest in between rounds. I'm really going somewhere with this. Your cornerman will keep you encouraged when you get tired. When I was growing up, I used to hear the mamas of the church say that every round goes higher and higher in the Lord. Well, if every round goes higher, then you will definitely need someone to remind you to keep going at times. So, your corner-man can't be just anybody. It probably will not be your best friend. It may not even be your mama or Father. It needs to be someone who is spiritually mature or seasoned in winning.

Let me pause for a moment. I need to point out that sometimes life is just what it is-life. Things happen in life. You may lose your job. That's life. You go on a few interviews, and you get another one. Or maybe you have a health condition due to you not eating properly. It happens. You change your diet, exercise, and if the condition has not gone too far, you get better. That's life. It is challenging, but you do what you must do to change the situation, and you move on. These mentioned challenges are not what I am speaking of in this portion of the book. I am speaking of an actual spiritual fight. If you are a believer in God's word, you will learn that your fight is not merely carnal but that there is spiritual warfare that happens. And although spiritual warfare is not seen with the natural eye and it is difficult to figure out, it is real. Therefore, you must learn your opponent.

There are several ways to learn about your opponent during spiritual warfare. One way is to get you some resources. One of the most beneficial resources for knowing your opponent that I found in the Bible. It is filled with words of life that will not only keep you encouraged during difficult times, but it will also teach you who you are fighting. In it, you will find that this fight started a long time ago and that many individuals before you were not only in this fight, but they won the fight. Here are a few scriptures located in the Bible that will help you understand who your opponent is:

1. "Be sober, be vigilant; because your adversary the devil, as a roaring lion, walketh about, seeking whom he may devour" (King James Version, n.d., 1 Peter 5:8)
2. "The thief cometh not, but for to steal, and to kill, and to destroy.." (King James Version, n.d., St. John 10:10)
3. "And the great dragon was cast out, that old serpent, called the Devil, and Satan, which deceiveth the whole world: he was cast out into the earth, and his angels were cast out with him." (King James Version, n.d., Revelations 12:9)

So, there you have it! Your opponent is not an obstacle. It is not a particular person. It is spiritual, and by now, you know that you can't fight in this spiritual war alone. But guess what? You do not have to. Now that you know who you are fighting, you are another step closer to winning. There is a man in the Bible named David. David went to battle against a Philistine champion who was considered to be a giant, but David was not threatened by his size. Instead, he studied his opponent. He knew the size of this giant could be used to HIS advantage. I used to hear the old folks say, "the bigger they are, the harder they fall." I believe this is how David thought. David may have been small in stature, but he was skilled in winning battles. His opponent came to battle with a sword and spear. David came to battle in the name of the Lord of hosts. So, with only a sling and stone, David was able to defeat the giant Philistine. He was able to do so because he understood what he was going up against, and he took God with him into the battle.

Now that you know who or what you are fighting, it will be important to keep your eye on It and not on distractions. If you focus on what is going wrong (distractions), then you do not see what is going right, and your growth is stunted. It is easy to get off track when you are in the ring because there is noise in the audience. Some people are cheering for you, telling you, "you can do it." Some people are cheering against you, saying, "It's not worth fighting for." Remember, the noise is just a distraction.

Do not let the noise from the audience keep you from hearing instructions from the referee (God). If you listen to the noise, you will forget the reason why you are fighting, and that is what your opponent wants you to do. But you are not ignorant of his tactics. In Matthew 14:18-21, Peter got distracted by the sound of the wind-the noise (King James Version, n.d.). He was doing fine until he forgot why he was on the water. Listening to the noise of your opponent will also cause you to doubt why you are fighting. You know you have a reason to keep fighting. Let me refresh your memory. Remember the one big dream you had? Yes, that one. Some time has passed but guess what? It can still come to fruition. It may tarry, but it will come to pass. Take it from someone who did not finish her undergraduate degree until I was in my forties. I obtained an associate degree and secured a job with benefits, but I started and stopped school so many times, listening to the noise of the audience, that it took what seemed like forever for my dream to come to pass. But I am a witness; even if it takes longer, it can still happen! Do not be tricked by the noise. If you can take just a moment to look backward and see how far you've come, you'll quickly realize just how strong you are, and the noise will become quieter.

Knowing your opponent means knowing yourself. When I was working on completing my undergraduate degree at the University of Wisconsin – Milwaukee, I had three children at home, worked a full-time job, and participated full-time in the ministry at my church. I was away from home at least three nights a week, trying to make it happen for my family. On many days I felt as if I was neglecting them. It seemed like no one understood that what I was doing was not a selfish move on my part, but in reality, it was a selfless move that would ultimately affect how we all lived. I was trying to make sure that my two girls knew what it looked like to work hard and beat the odds that were stacked against me. I was trying to care for my elderly mama, who was in and out of the hospital at this time, and I was trying to keep good grades so that I would be eligible for scholarships and tuition reimbursement. Who wants to owe a ton of money back after graduation? All of this left me in tears many nights. I did not let others see the tears. I just knew I had to keep fighting. I noted this to encourage you. Even with tears in your eyes, keep fighting! Even if no one understands, keep fighting!

One night I had a dream, and in this dream, I was quoting this scripture "Behold, I give unto you power to tread on serpents and scorpions and over all the power of the enemy: and nothing by any means shall hurt you" (King James Version, n.d., Luke 10:19). After dreaming this, I knew that my strength had been renewed and that I must continue to see what the end was going to be. I knew that if God took the time to show me in a dream that I possessed power, which I knew nothing about, that I would be straight! No matter who supported or agreed with me. No matter if my children could see the big picture at the time or not.

This power to tread on serpents meant that even if the situation appeared life-threatening, I could still win even if my opponent seemed to outweigh me, even when my body was tired, even when things became hectic on my job, and even when it felt like I was being stretched to the max. I could not let the stress of it all overtake me because God had given me power. BUT, I had to use the power that was in me to fight. This is what you will need to do, as well. Realize the power that is within you to recognize your opponent and then use it. God did not give you this power to go to waste. He knew your opponent was going to put roadblocks in the way, so he gave you the power to overcome them. Stay focused, get back in the ring, and keep fighting!

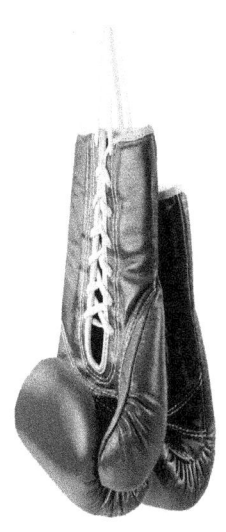

Strategy #4
Rest Breaks

A Song for this Moment:

Hang On (remix), Pastor Marlon Lock

You have been in training; you have a good regimen in place now. You know what you are up against. Your strength has been renewed, and you got a couple of punches in. Now it is time to enjoy the hard work. All work and no play isn't good for anyone. You deserve a break. First, we must give honor where honor is due. To God, be the glory for the things He has done! Although this round may be over, and you will still need to fight at times, you can rest for a moment knowing that you are fighting a good fight.

A trained boxer knows he must take rest breaks in between rounds. You must take the time to look back and see how far you have come. Maybe you started the fight unemployed or working paycheck to paycheck as I did, but you have now decided to finish that degree that you started years ago. Get excited about the decision you have made. Do not focus on how hard it will be to accomplish the goal. Focus on the fact that you called the University of your choice and made an appointment to enroll! Focus on the fact that you just got your letter of acceptance! Focus on your latter days will be greater than your former days! Focus on that "A" that you earned on your first report card.

Celebrate your new mindset. You may have started off with a deficit mindset. Always saying "I Can't" or finding a reason not to start something, but now you find yourself taking a chance! Now, you find yourself building on existing strength! Now, your first semester at your choice University is complete! Now, you have landed that job you've been wanting! You may not be where you thought you would be at this point in your life but listen, my friend, you are not where you started. Celebrate! There is a proverb in which the original origin is unknown that says, "all work and no plays makes Jack a dull boy." It is time to play!

If you have been working hard, you deserve to kick your feet up and chill. Or if chillin' is not your thing, then dance. I remember when I started fighting, I didn't have much extra money to splurge (remember I had children and was living paycheck to paycheck), so I would schedule "girls night out" with my three accountability partners (Sherry, Alicia, and Winifred). We would do this about every three months. We would have a night out on the town just to catch up, laugh, and discuss our next moves. We were all fighting something, so we all celebrated together. Sometimes we would pick an upscale restaurant such as Capital Grille or Mo's Steakhouse located in downtown Milwaukee. We would step out of our "fighting" gear and put on some heels and a cute outfit, and have ourselves a good time. Now, it was not always an upscale celebration. Sometimes, we would just get in the truck and drive to a nearby shopping outlet. Those drives allowed us to chat, laugh, and strengthen each other.

You may be an introvert, so it may be quiet time alone in a room full of candles or going to the Spa for a much-needed reflexology massage. Maybe it is just walking through the mall with your bag of Buddy Squirrel cheese and caramel mixed popcorn. The point is, whatever resting from your hard work and celebrating means to you, then do it.

I learned that when boxers are training to fight, they are allowed what is called a rest day. The rest day allows their body to consolidate the hard work they were doing. The rest days are when the muscles can recover and become stronger so the nervous system can have a chance to regenerate. I'm going somewhere with this. You are now a fighter! You will need to give your mind a chance to recoup. Training, fighting, or working every day with no rest days will cause more of a strain on you than when you started. It will cause you to become overwhelmed. And you do not want to do that because you have more fighting to do. Take this time to start thinking about some ways or someplace that you enjoy and could use as your "night out on the town" or recouping days.

"Surround yourself with people who have dreams, desire and ambition; They'll help you push for and realize your own."

KUSHANDWIZDOM

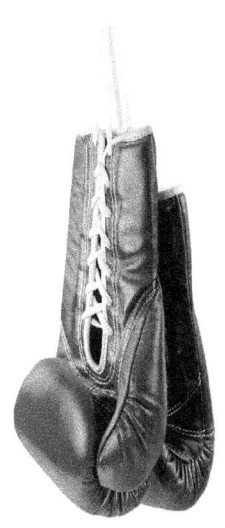

Strategy #5
Stay Focused

A Song for this Moment:

*Blessings On Blessings (The B.O.B Bounce)
by Anthony Brown & Group Therapy*

The closer you get to winning the championship, the more distractions will come. But guess what? You are still going to win! I must be honest. There were times when I became weary. I definitely do not want you to get the impression that because I am a fighter that I never fainted. Or because I am sharing the strategies that helped me come out with my hands up with you, that it was all peaches and cream. That was not the case at all. I can remember my darkest moment as if it were yesterday. It was in 2003. Sitting on my sofa, I was bent over with my head in my lap and tears rolling down my face. And even though I did not know what a nervous breakdown felt like, I had heard the term before and thought for sure I was going to have one. The thing is, as we navigate this thing called life, we make decisions based on our previous experiences. We do not always make the best decisions, but it is no fault of our own. It's just how it goes. Some of the decisions I had made were not the best ones, and I was now in a situation where I felt as if I was stuck. I had been the "strong" one for so long till I was tired of being strong, and I had a full-blown meltdown. Yes, a meltdown. Just like a toddler who is fighting their sleep. It was not a nervous breakdown at all. I was just exhausted. I had been fighting for and with others for so long till I fainted. Let us talk about this for a moment.

Fighting for others

Sometimes when you are the "strong" one, people seem to use your strength instead of their own. They call on you when there is trouble in the family. They call on you when there is an issue at work, hoping you will speak up for the team at the professional development meeting, and they may even call on you when there is an issue at church. Why? Because they know you are the one who will speak up at the auxiliary meeting. What they do not know is, yes, you may speak up, but it is only because you have a desire to resolve and live in peace. It is not because you desire to be confrontational.

I had to stop allowing people to use my voice (strength) and teach them how to use their own because all the while they were calling on me, I was slowly fainting. I was fainting because the strength that I had was being inappropriately utilized, and instead of being strengthened, I was becoming weak. If this has happened or happens to you, you can rest assured that because you have come this far, that you will get through this season. This feeling of exhaustion will not last forever.

For my Bible readers

In the book of Galatians 6:9, it reads, "Let us not be weary in well doing: for in due season, we shall reap if we faint not" (King James Version, n.d.). This scripture was written just for you. Think about it. God had you in mind before you were even born. He knew at some point in your life's journey, you would feel this way, so he inspired a man (Paul) to put these words together to help you when you needed it the most. Yes, my friend, fighting is exhausting. But if you are fighting for your life and the life of your children, then it is a good fight, and you must not lose hope. When you come to a moment of exhaustion, as I did, remember that you gain strength and endurance after every round. You cannot stop now.

There is another scripture in the Bible that says if you wait on the Lord, you will gain new strength; you will mount up with wings like eagles. Wow, that is pretty deep to consider. In those weary moments, all you must do is rest in God's care. Then Isaiah 40:31 goes on to say that you will "run and not get weary" and "walk and not faint" (King James Version, n.d.). The reason you will not faint is that you have allowed God to take some of the pressure that was causing you to become tired, and now your load is feeling lighter. You can continue to see what the end is going to be. You must know that God gives strength to the weary! So, it is okay if you get tired every now and then. Just do not stay stuck. Get back up and get back in the ring. You have a championship to win.

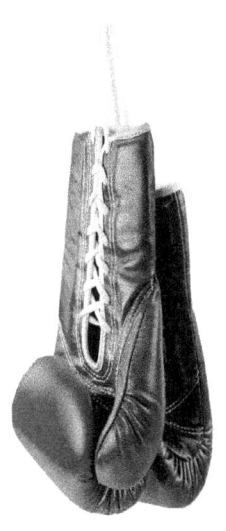

Strategy #6
Don't Let the War Wounds Fool You

A Song for this Moment:

I Got That (Remix Audio) ft. 1K Phew- by Anthony Brown & Group Therapy

I know right about now you are feeling more confident. I mean, who wouldn't. You have built endurance, and you have been using these strategies to overcome opposition, and it is working. I told you that you had an inner strength that you did not even know was there. I know that I am not the only person that was born into a family of fighters. I know I am not the only person whose momma taught them how to fight. Sometimes we just need someone to ignite the fire. Now that you have got yourself together let's finish this fight with integrity.

In the world of boxing, the day after a victory, it is expected that you will have some soreness, some bruising, and maybe even some bumps from the intensity of the fight. But that is okay; that is just the proof that you stayed to the course and gave it all you had. Those are just war wounds, and every champion has them.

This last round may be the most difficult one, but it also must be the most strategic one. Why, because your opponent (whatever or whoever it may be) has had time to study your footwork and your handwork. So, you must always keep a couple of surprises up your sleeve. You will need to think smart. Just as you have been studied, you have also been able to study patterns of whatever or whoever you are fighting against. The Bible tells us that there is no new thing under the sun (Ecclesiastes 1:9). This means nothing should catch you by surprise. Go into this last round with a competitive mindset. I mean, you do want to win, right? Go into this last round with the mindset that you are taking over territories, and everything you may have lost in any other round will be conquered in this one. Go into this last round, knowing that it didn't beat you last time, and it won't beat you this time. Go into this last round with a fervent prayer and some blessed oil. If you have not prayed any other round, you better pray this one.

Remember How You Got the War Wounds

This is the time for you to remember *how* you got those war wounds. I can remember when I got a couple of my war wounds (scars). I was newly married, expecting a child, and my husband and I were living in separate houses. Yes, we were separated during my pregnancy. Who does that, right? I was embarrassed, to say the least. Here I was, married, and going to my doctor's appointments by myself as if I were single. All I could think was, how did I get here, and man, oh man, I did not sign up for this.

It was a high-risk pregnancy, so I probably had more appointments than someone with a normal pregnancy would have. One night I experienced some complications that caused me to end up in the emergency room. I had to go alone. I was so hurt. I was wounded. I was lying on the hospital bed, talking to someone other than my husband. They were praying and comforting me, but again, it was not the man whose child I was carrying. I thank God for the prayer of my mentor, but can you imagine the turmoil I experienced to even need to call her? But guess what, I made it through that season. I got through the high-risk pregnancy. I had a healthy baby and moved forward. You may have experienced loneliness or rejection as well. You may even be experiencing it right now, but if I could make it through, you for sure can and will too.

There will be visible scars. Although the wound is healed, the scar is still visible. Do not get me wrong, I would not wish that experience on anyone but consider this, what doesn't kill you, will only make you stronger. War wounds are on the outside. They are visible to people. But all the while, people are looking at the outward appearance. You, my friend, are being made stronger. It may look like you are defeated, but it looked like Jesus was too. With nail prints in his hands and stripes all over his body, he was counted out by many. He endured hardship, temptation, and even wrongful judgment. But those war wounds were part of the process, just like mine and yours are. I shared this part of my life with you because it is one of my most horrendous moments ever. I wanted to be transparent, so you know that you are not the only one with war wounds.

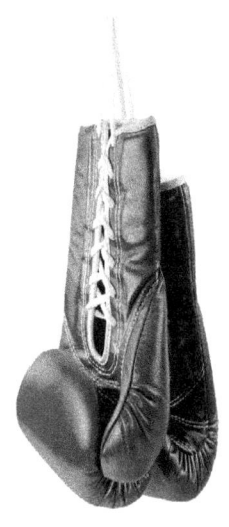

Tender Spots

You may still have some tender spots or scabs that you are still picking at. Leave the scabs alone, or they will never heal. Some of our war wounds come from our poor choices. Maybe the soreness in this round may have come from not listening to the Holy Spirit when he told you to flee from that toxic relationship, and it took you an extra year-but you left. Your bruises may have come from that time when you were turned down for the job which you had been trying to get for so long. You were hurt and left feeling defeated. Maybe being a single parent left you with a bump or two, but that is okay. Soon those ashes will be turned into beauty, and your testimony will be all that others see. I know from experience that some issues are more difficult than others to fight through. Here me when I say this, there is nothing too hard for God. You know how when you are experiencing some aches or stiffness in your physical body, and you go to get a deep tissue massage to release the tension that has built up? Well, that is what God does when you are fighting, and you experience pain that lingers. He releases tension, anxiety, and even depression. If you are willing to release the tension (tender spots), he can heal. As a matter of fact, the Bible says in 1 Peter 5:7 to "cast all your cares upon him because he cares for you" (*King James Version*, n.d.). I heard someone say that time heals all wounds. I would like to add that time ***with God*** heals all wounds. It may take some time before you are pain-free but know that you will be free indeed.

"Tears are prayers too. they travel to God when we can't speak."

Psalms 56:8

Don't Take it Personal

Now here is where you know that you know, that you know that you've come out with your hands up-- When you no longer look for others to celebrate you. This was the moment when I knew I was "grown." It was when I stopped looking for people to pat me on the back. Being the baby girl of my family, I was used to being celebrated. When I became an adult, I expected it. Let me tell you, though. It can be one of the biggest disappointments in life. And if not careful, it can cause you to resort back to a deficit mindset. You may be the person who enjoys celebrating with others. You may show up at every birthday celebration you are invited to, every graduation ceremony, and even every wedding.

Just in case it is not reciprocated, I want you to finish this book knowing that you are a "boss," regardless of the applause. I know we expect our family to support our every endeavor. You may also expect your church-family to support your accomplishments. I mean, when you were walking around with your head down, everybody had something to say, so of course, you would expect the applause when you actually win. I did! Well, the truth is, it does not always happen. Don't take it personally. You must go into this fight, understanding that you are building character and sometimes who you are becoming is intimidating to others – to the point where they are stuck trying to figure out how you did it, instead of celebrating that you did it. You look new. You smell new, and you are going to new places. They are perplexed. You did a 180-degree spin on them. Yes, I mean a 180-degree spin and not a 360, because if you do a 360-degree spin, then you end up right back where you started. It's not that they wanted to see you faint, but it happened so quickly, they just forgot to clap. Clap for yourself! Now, this does not give you the right to walk around with a chip on your shoulder. Victory looks good on you but remember the glory belongs to God. People do not see the sleepless nights, the intense prayers, or any of the struggles you had to endure during this process, and that is okay.

Do not put your hope in people. Do not let the lack of response from others discourage you. Remember, you were not doing it for them anyway. You were fighting because you realized that your life was purposeful. You were fighting because the opposition had you bound. You were fighting because you decided that your fate was not in the hands of anyone else, but it was in the hands of God. You were fighting because your children needed you to model what winning looks like. You were not fighting to be congratulated. You were fighting to win.

Trust me; there is somebody rooting for you. Even if it is not the person, you expected. Your children, although when they are young, do not always appreciate or celebrate you. When they get older, they will. You have seen it time and time again. Adult children give recognition to their parents for the sacrifices and the strong foundation that was laid for them. That is going to be you one day. Think about your job. They cannot ignore your attributes to the company for too long. You will be offered a raise in the salary you deserve. It just may not come when you expect it. There is somebody that you did not even know was watching you that is waiting to celebrate you. Just continue to lift your head, regardless of the applause.

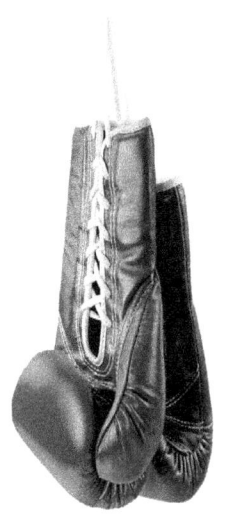

What's Next?
It's in Your Words

Winning comes with great responsibility. There is someone else that needs to hear your testimony. Seize the opportunity to tell your story. You have discovered, the God that is within you is bigger than any obstacle. You did not let the size of the giant intimidate you. When you saw trouble coming, you did not run or hide. Instead, you faced it head-on. You did not doubt God's promises. You remembered the purpose over the pressure. Do not be afraid to share your story.

This part is for my ladies. I know you have been hurt before, but you must learn how to be in a relationship with other women. We need each other. We are stronger together. There is power in numbers. God never intended for you to walk alone. Now that you have gotten past the lack of applause learn to trust again. It is the only way the winning cycle can continue. Understand, it is a blessing to be a blessing to others. Do not be hesitant to spread the good news. It's the garbage that you don't want to spread or the deficit language that you don't want to speak. You already know that life and death lie within the power of the tongue. So, say something powerful. Say something impactful. Say something that will change somebody else's life. You won! Do not worry about if people think you are boasting. Nope, you are not boasting about yourself. You are sharing to build someone else up. Iron sharpens iron.

> *"As iron sharpens iron,*
> *so a friend sharpens a friend."*
> *Proverbs 27:17 (NLT)*

Whatever platform you have been given, use it to help someone else win. It may be the women's group at a local church. It could be a local youth mentorship club. It could even be through a podcast of some sort. Do not underestimate the power of your words. Use what you have learned to go back to the "projects" and show somebody else how to come out. Let us think about this, of all the situations you have fought through, what is one of the most memorable victories? Okay, now use that! Did you make it through a divorce? If so, make sure when you encounter another individual going through the same thing, you share your story.

Their victory may be dependent on your voice. I am reminded of a young man in the Bible by the name of Joseph. Because of jealousy, Joseph was stripped of the colorful coat that had been given to him by his father and thrown in a pit by his own brothers

(King James Version, n.d.). Here goes opposition. God did not leave Joseph in the pit. God was with Joseph. Joseph was pulled out of the pit and some years later ended up in prison on false accusations. More opposition. Once again, God was with Joseph, even in prison. Joseph ended up in a palace with the title of governor. So, from the pit to prison, to the palace, now, Joseph had a platform. That very same platform allowed him the opportunity to forgive and feed the very same people who threw him in the pit. Joseph used his platform for good. After all, it was God who carried him through. I have condensed this history and example of Joseph for the sake of this book, but I encourage you to read Genesis chapters 37-42. I mentioned this illustration to let you see that every opposition that you have faced had a purpose.

The very fact that you made it through is evidence of that. Now that you are in the palace use your platform to pull someone else out of the pit or out of prison. "Feed," the people who the opposition came through. This is how God gets the glory.

From My Heart To Yours

When I started writing this book, I was anxious to get it done. I had heard from God and knew it was His will for my life. I was willing to do what pleased Him. I thought that because it was His will that everything would go smoothly. I was wrong. As much as I knew it was part of God's plan for my life, I had forgotten just that quick how the opposition was waiting on the other side. I started off strong, and then I drew a blank. At some moments, I could not see how I would finish. I cried, I complained, and I fussed at the kids. I confess. I probably did not handle everything perfectly.

There were many sleepless nights, but I had to fight to get to the end. I learned a few things during this fight to finish. I learned that patience is a virtue. Yes, I had to wait on the words that I was writing to be perfected in my heart. I wanted to be finished because my vision was past where I was actually at. I could see the finish line, but I needed to work to get there. Someone once told me, slow and steady wins the race, and now I know that to be true. I remembered that at the beginning of this year, our churches' new year theme was 20/20 vision. I had to remind myself to focus on the "Why." You see, my "Why" was bigger than just producing a book. My "Why" was not selfish. My "Why" wanted to impact the world, and so, I pressed through the exhaustion. I would set my alarm clock at midnight so that my house was quiet, and I could hear from God.

Setting my clock for midnight meant I was up until 3 a.m. some mornings. Coffee became my best friend. I had something in view, and it took sacrifice. I share my heart with you at this moment because maybe you are not writing a book, but you are battling between purpose and pleasure. Maybe you are stuck and don't quite know how to maneuver through. I suggest that you go back to the drawing board. When you go back to the drawing board, you will remember your "Why."

"A winner is a dreamer that never gives up."
Nelson Mandela

A List For My Ladies

I have created this list, which includes common areas we often fight or fight through. Feel free to add to the list to make it personal for you. I am asking you to cross off each area as you begin to Win in the given area. The intent is for you to see how far you have come in your journey.

1. Abandonment

2. Low self-esteem

3. Guilt

4. Broken Relationships (divorce, friendships, etc.)

5. Loneliness

6. Poverty

7.

8.

9.

10.

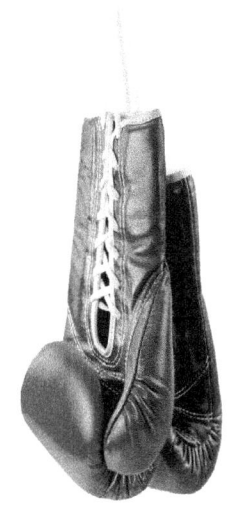

A List For My Fellas

I have created this list, which includes common areas we often fight or fight through. Feel free to add to the list to make it personal for you. I am asking you to cross off each area as you begin to Win in the given area. The intent is for you to see how far you have come in your journey.

1. Systematic Obstacles

2. Financial Hardship

3. Broken Relationships (divorce, children, etc.)

4. Unforgiveness

5. Self-Worth

6. Fleshly Desires (sex before marriage, adultery, faithfulness, etc.)

7.

8.

9.

10.

A Prayer For The Fighter In You

Dear Heavenly Father, I take this moment to thank you for this reader who decided to Fight and not Faint. I pray that after they read this book, that their desire to obtain a more intimate relationship with you has been ignited. I ask you, Father, to renew their strength and rebuild them where they may have been torn down. I ask that you whisper sweet words to their spirit and let them know that your love for them is unfailing and that your Holy Spirit is a comforter and a keeper. I ask that you give them a spirit of discernment so that nothing can sneak up on them or catch them by surprise so that they are ready to conquer the world. I ask that you assure them that everything they need to Win, is already within them because you have already given them the tools. Let them understand that they are not fighting alone and that you will be there every step of the way if they acknowledge you. Father, because they have decided to be a blessing to me, your daughter, I ask that you enlarge their territory and bless their going out and their coming in. Give them the power to get wealth, oh God. Bless their family. Bless their finances and give them opportunities to succeed. Let your power fall on them to enable them to be victorious in all they set to do that is according to your will.
I pray this prayer and all others in the name of Jesus,
Amen

www.ingramcontent.com/pod-product-compliance
Lightning Source LLC
Chambersburg PA
CBHW050041080526
44586CB00014B/1407